THE BEATLES
Sheet Music Collection

Cover photo: Getty Images / Central Press / Stringer

ISBN 978-1-4950-9603-7

HAL•LEONARD®

7777 W. BLUEMOUND RD. P.O. BOX 13819 MILWAUKEE, WI 53213

In Australia Contact:
Hal Leonard Australia Pty. Ltd.
4 Lentara Court
Cheltenham, Victoria, 3192 Australia
Email: ausadmin@halleonard.com.au

Visit Hal Leonard Online at
www.halleonard.com

THE BEATLES
Sheet Music Collection

* *Abbey Road* medley

ACROSS THE UNIVERSE

Words and Music by JOHN LENNON
and PAUL McCARTNEY

Words are flow-ing out __ like end-less rain __ in-to a pa-per cup, __ they
slith-er while _ they pass, they slip a-way __ a-cross the u-ni-verse. _
Pools of sor-row, waves of joy are drift-ing through my o-pened mind, _ pos-

ALL MY LOVING

Words and Music by JOHN LENNON
and PAUL McCARTNEY

ALL YOU NEED IS LOVE

Words and Music by JOHN LENNON
and PAUL McCARTNEY

THE BALLAD OF JOHN AND YOKO

Words and Music by JOHN LENNON
and PAUL McCARTNEY

Moderate Rock

Stand-ing in the dock at South-amp-
Fin-'lly made the plane in-to Par-
Par-is to the Am-ster-dam Hil-

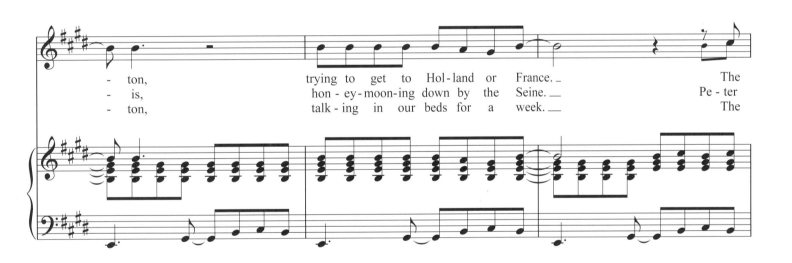

-ton,   trying to get to Hol-land or France. ___ The
-is,   hon-ey-moon-ing down by the Seine. ___ The Pe-ter
-ton,   talk-ing in our beds for a week. ___ The

man in the mac ___ said, ___ "You've got to go back." ___ You know they
Brown called to say, ___ "You ___ can make it O - K. ___ You can get
news-peo-ple said, ___ "Say, what're you do-ing in bed?" ___ I said, "We're

Sav-ing up your mon-ey for a rain - y day,

giv-ing all your clothes to char - i - ty.

Last night the wife said,

"Oh boy, when you're dead, you don't take noth-ing with you but your soul." _____ Think!

Made a light-ning trip to Vi - en - na,
Caught the ear - ly plane back to Lon - don,

AND I LOVE HER

Words and Music by JOHN LENNON
and PAUL McCARTNEY

End instrumental solo

And I love

her.

BACK IN THE U.S.S.R.

Words and Music by JOHN LENNON
and PAUL McCARTNEY

Flew in from Mi - a - mi Beach, B.
Been a - way so long I hard - ly
Show me 'round your snow - peaked moun - tains

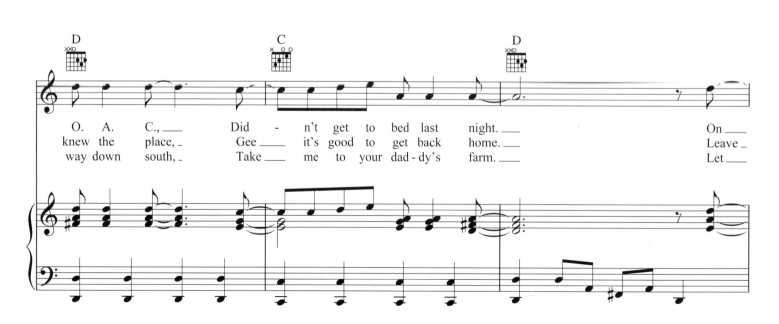

O. A. C., _____ Did - n't get to bed last night. _____ On _____
knew the place, _ Gee _____ it's good to get back home. _____ Leave _____
way down south, _ Take _____ me to your dad - dy's farm. _____ Let _____

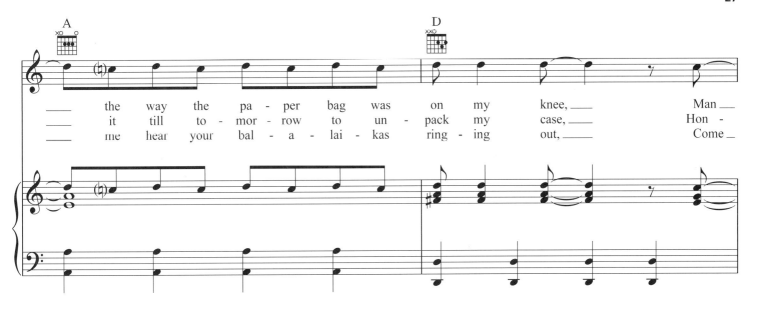

the way the pa - per bag was on my knee, ____ Man ____
it till to - mor - row to un - pack my case, ____ Hon -
me hear your bal - a - lai - kas ring - ing out, ____ Come ____

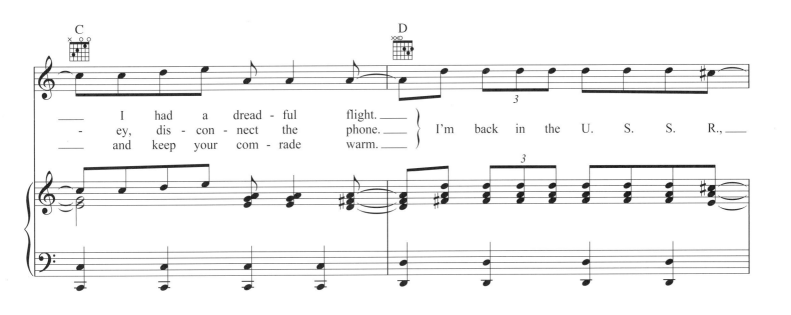

____ I had a dread - ful flight. ____
- ey, dis - con - nect the phone. ____
____ and keep your com - rade warm. ____
I'm back in the U. S. S. R., ____

You don't __ know how luck - y you are, ____ boy. __

To Coda

BECAUSE

Words and Music by JOHN LENNON
and PAUL McCARTNEY

BEING FOR THE BENEFIT OF MR. KITE

Words and Music by JOHN LENNON
and PAUL McCARTNEY

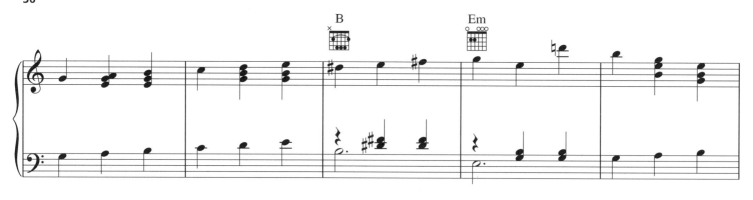

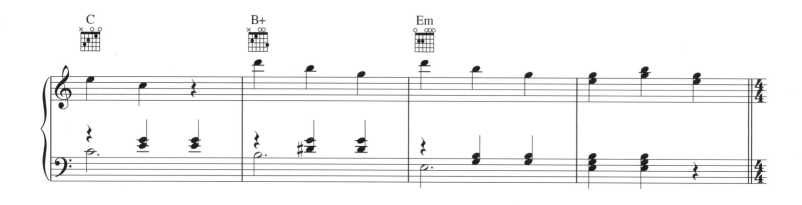

Original tempo

D.S. al Coda

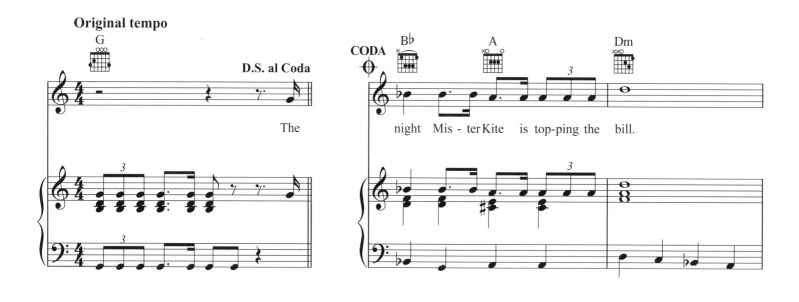

The night Mis - ter Kite is top-ping the bill.

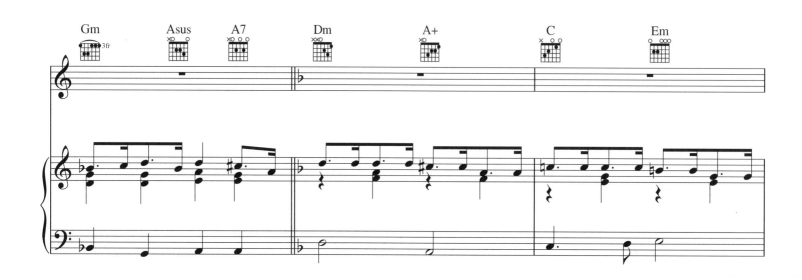

BIRTHDAY

Words and Music by JOHN LENNON
and PAUL McCARTNEY

Moderately fast Rock

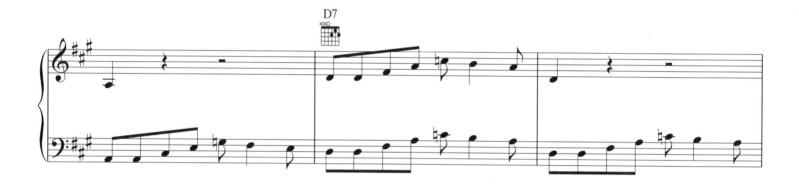

You say it's your birth - day,

BLACKBIRD

Words and Music by JOHN LENNON
and PAUL McCARTNEY

Slowly and smoothly

Black-bird sing-ing in the dead of night, _
Black-bird sing-ing in the dead of night, _

take these bro-ken wings _ and learn to fly; _
take these sunk-en eyes _ and learn to see; _

all your life _____ you were on-ly wait-ing for this mo-ment to a -
all your life _____ you were on-ly wait-ing for this mo-ment to be

CAN'T BUY ME LOVE

Words and Music by JOHN LENNON
and PAUL McCARTNEY

Can't buy me love, _____ oh, _____ love _

_____ oh, _____ can't buy me love, _____ oh. _____ I'll

buy you a dia-mond ring, ___ my friend, _ if it makes you feel al-right, _
give you ___ all I've got ___ to give ___ if you say you love me too, _

Instrumental solo

D.S. al Coda
(take 2nd ending)

COME TOGETHER

Words and Music by JOHN LENNON
and PAUL McCARTNEY

DEAR PRUDENCE

Words and Music by JOHN LENNON
and PAUL McCARTNEY

Dear _____ Pru - dence, _____
_____ Pru - dence, _____
_____ Pru - dence, _____

won't you come out to play? _____
o - pen up _____ your eyes. _____
let me see _____ you smile. _____

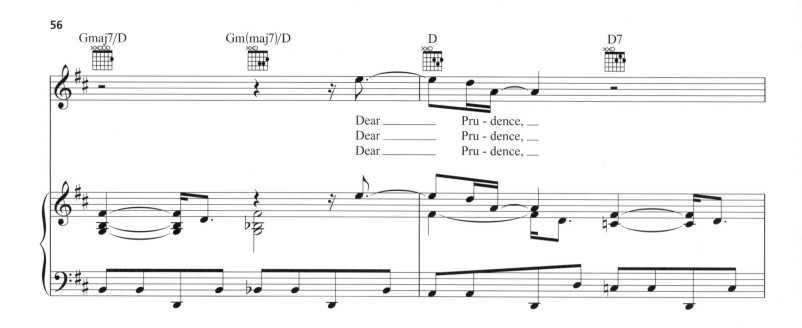

Dear _____ Pru - dence, __
Dear _____ Pru - dence, __
Dear _____ Pru - dence, __

greet the brand - new day. _____
see the sun - ny skies. _____
like a lit - tle child. _____

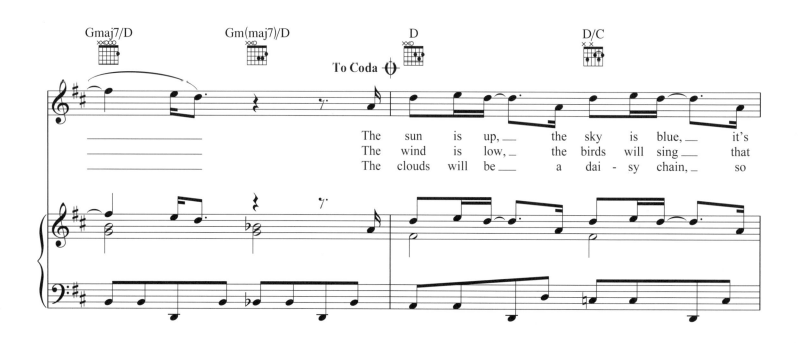

To Coda

The sun is up, __ the sky is blue, __ it's
The wind is low, __ the birds will sing __ that
The clouds will be __ a dai - sy chain, __ so

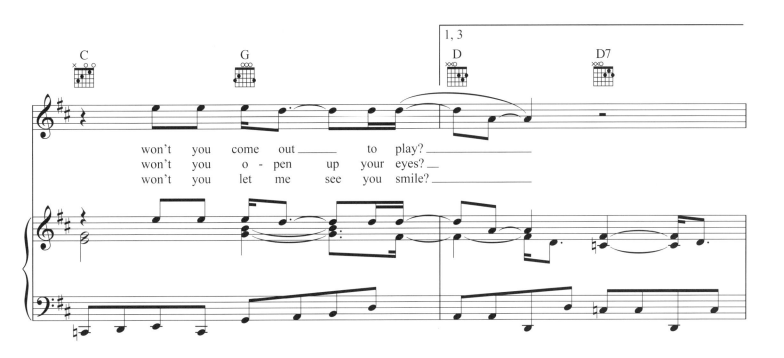

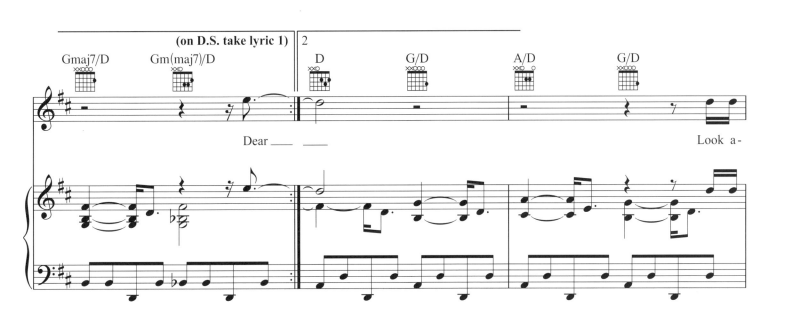

A DAY IN THE LIFE

Words and Music by JOHN LENNON
and PAUL McCARTNEY

DO YOU WANT TO KNOW A SECRET?

Words and Music by JOHN LENNON
and PAUL McCARTNEY

I've known the se-cret for a week or two, ____

no - bod - y knows, just we two. ____

D.S. al Coda

CODA

Repeat and Fade | **Optional Ending**

Ooh. Ooh. ____

DON'T LET ME DOWN

Words and Music by JOHN LENNON
and PAUL McCARTNEY

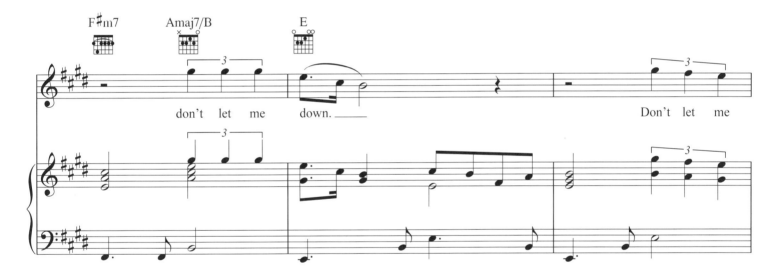

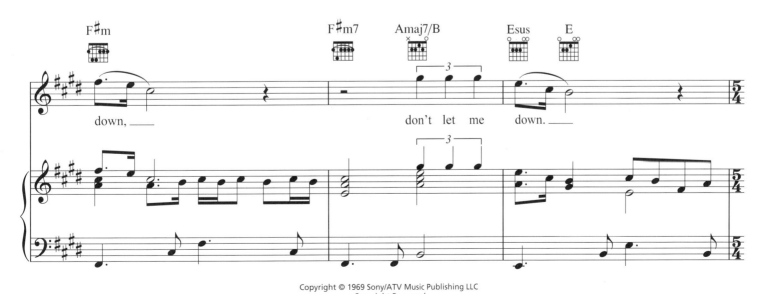

DRIVE MY CAR

Words and Music by JOHN LENNON
and PAUL McCARTNEY

FIXING A HOLE

Words and Music by JOHN LENNON
and PAUL McCARTNEY

EIGHT DAYS A WEEK

Words and Music by JOHN LENNON
and PAUL McCARTNEY

ELEANOR RIGBY

Words and Music by JOHN LENNON
and PAUL McCARTNEY

Moderately, with a steady beat

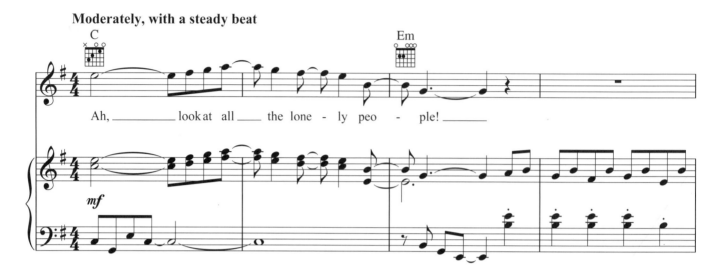

Ah, _____ look at all _____ the lone - ly peo - ple! _____

Ah, _____ look at all _____ the lone - ly peo - ple! _____

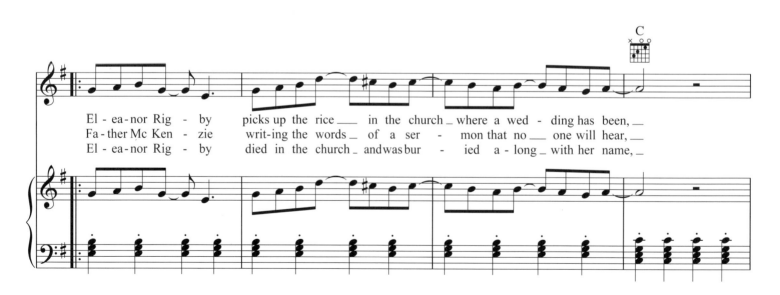

El - ea - nor Rig - by   picks up the rice _____ in the church _____ where a wed - ding has been, _____
Fa - ther Mc Ken - zie   writ - ing the words _____ of a ser - mon that no _____ one will hear, _____
El - ea - nor Rig - by   died in the church _____ and was bur - ied a - long _____ with her name, _____

THE FOOL ON THE HILL

Words and Music by JOHN LENNON
and PAUL McCARTNEY

Day af-ter day, a-lone on a hill, the
Well on the way, head in a cloud, the

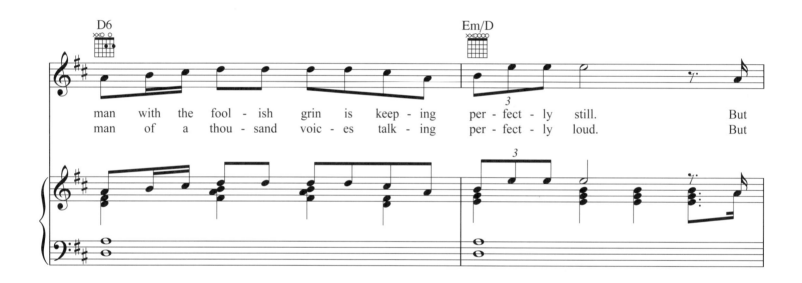

man with the fool-ish grin is keep-ing per-fect-ly still. But
man of a thou-sand voic-es talk-ing per-fect-ly loud. But

no-bod-y wants to know him, they can see that he's just a fool. And
no-bod-y ev-er hears him, or the sound he ap-pears to make. And

FOR NO ONE

Words and Music by JOHN LENNON
and PAUL McCARTNEY

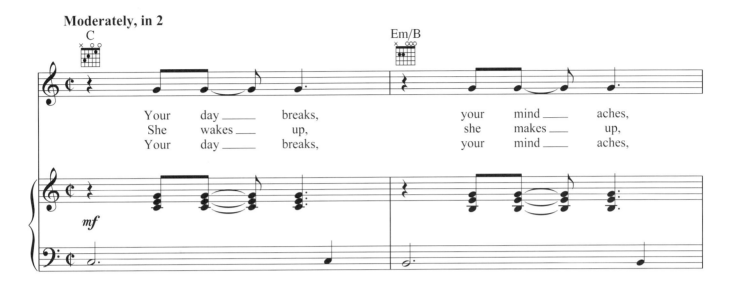

Moderately, in 2

Your day _____ breaks, your mind _____ aches,
She wakes _____ up, she makes _____ up,
Your day _____ breaks, your mind _____ aches,

you find _____ that all _____ her words of kind - ness lin - ger on _____
she takes _____ her time _____ and does - n't feel she has to hur -
there will _____ be times _____ when all the things she said will fill _____

_____ when she no long - er needs _____ you. _____
- ry; she no long - er needs _____ you. _____
_____ your head; you won't for - get _____ her.

FROM ME TO YOU

Words and Music by JOHN LENNON
and PAUL McCARTNEY

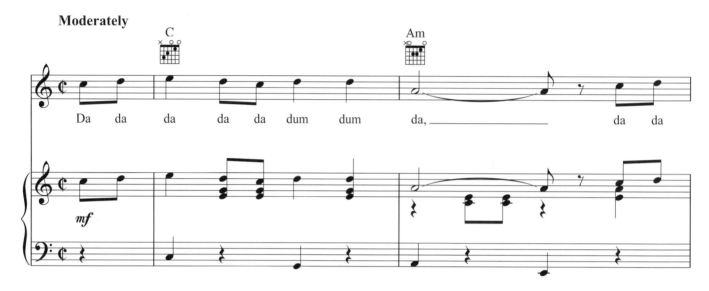

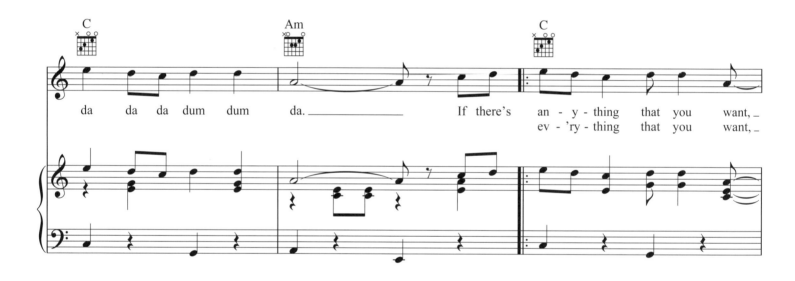

GET BACK

Words and Music by JOHN LENNON
and PAUL McCARTNEY

Jo Jo was a man who thought _ he was a lon - er, but _
Instrumental
Sweet Lor - et - ta Mar - tin thought _ she was a wom - an, but _
Instrumental

_ he knew it could - n't last. _
_ she was an - oth - er man. _

Jo _ Jo left his home in Tuc -
All _ the girls a - round her say _

(Get back, Jo Jo)

Spoken ad lib:

Get back, Loretta, your momma's waitin' for you
Wearin' her high heel shoes and a low neck sweater.
Get back home, Loretta.

Repeat and Fade

GIRL

Words and Music by JOHN LENNON
and PAUL McCARTNEY

Is there an-y-bod-y going to lis-ten to my sto-ry,
think of all the times I tried so hard to leave her,
told when she was young that pain would lead to pleas-ure?

all a-bout the girl who came to stay?
she will turn to me and start to cry.
Did she un-der-stand it when they said

She's the kind of girl you want so much it
And she prom-is-es the earth to me and
that a man must break his back to earn his

makes you sor-ry,
I be-lieve her,
day of lei-sure?

still, you don't re-gret a sin-gle day.
af-ter all this time I don't know why.
Will she still be-lieve it when he's dead?

To Coda

Ah,

GETTING BETTER

Words and Music by JOHN LENNON
and PAUL McCARTNEY

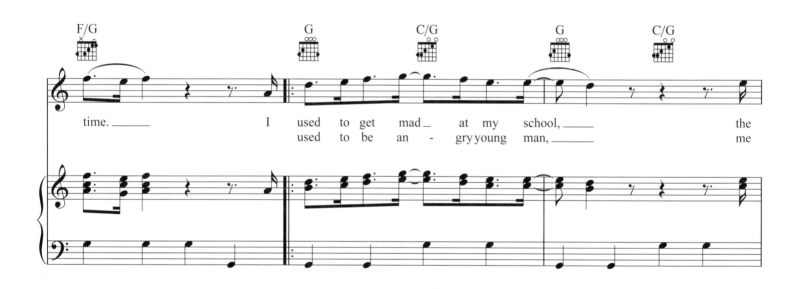

GOOD DAY SUNSHINE

Words and Music by JOHN LENNON
and PAUL McCARTNEY

GOOD NIGHT

Words and Music by JOHN LENNON
and PAUL McCARTNEY

GOT TO GET YOU INTO MY LIFE

Words and Music by JOHN LENNON
and PAUL McCARTNEY

I was a-lone, __ I took a ride, __ I did-n't know __ what I would find __
You did-n't run, __ you did-n't lie, __ you knew I want-ed just to hold __
What can I do, __ what can I be? __ When I'm with you, __ I want to stay __

__ there. __
__ you. __
__ there. __

An-oth-er road __ where may-be I __
And had you gone, __ you knew in time __
If I'm true __ I'll nev-er leave, __

could see an-oth-er kind of mind ___ there. ___
we'd meet a-gain, for I had told ___ you. ___
and if I do, ___ I know the way ___ there. ___

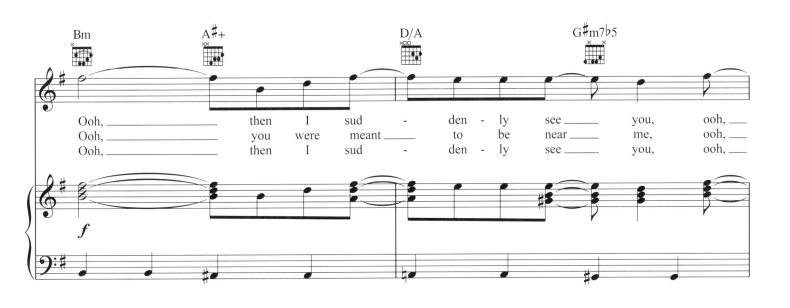

Ooh, _____ then I sud-den-ly see ___ you, ooh, ___
Ooh, _____ you were meant ___ to be near ___ me, ooh, ___
Ooh, _____ then I sud-den-ly see ___ you, ooh, ___

_____ did I tell ___ you I need ___ you ev-'ry sin-gle
_____ and I want ___ you to hear ___ me say we'll be to-
_____ did I tell ___ you I need ___ you ev-'ry sin-gle

Got to get you in - to my life! _

Repeat and Fade

A HARD DAY'S NIGHT

Words and Music by JOHN LENNON
and PAUL McCARTNEY

Moderately, with a beat

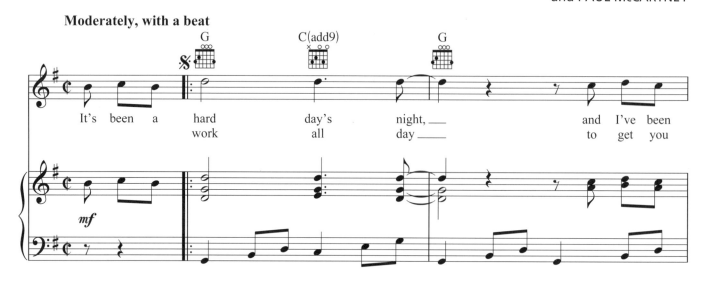

It's been a hard day's night, ___ and I've been
work all day ___ to get you

work-ing like a dog. ___ It's been a hard day's night, ___
mon-ey to buy your things. ___ And it's worth it just to hear you say ___

___ I should be sleep-ing like a log. ___ But when I
___ you're gon-na give me ev-'ry-thing. ___ So why on

HELLO, GOODBYE

Words and Music by JOHN LENNON
and PAUL McCARTNEY

Moderately

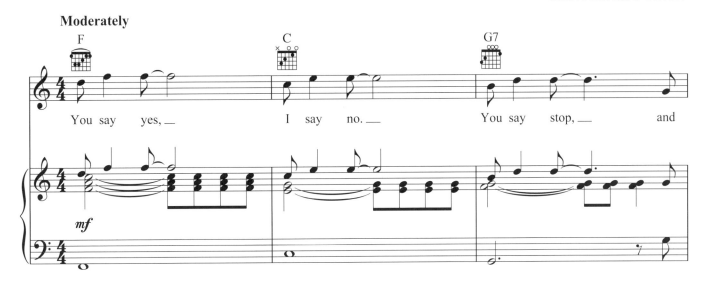

You say yes, __ I say no. __ You say stop, __ and

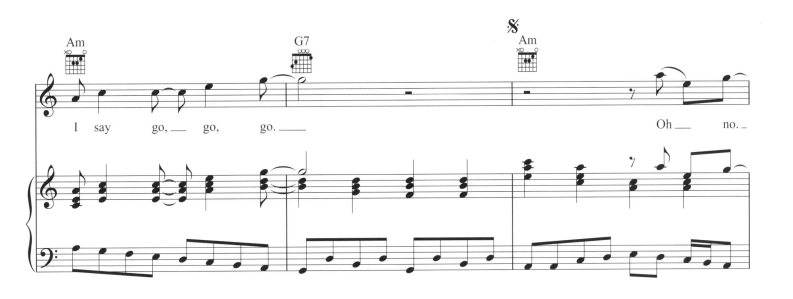

I say go, __ go, go. __ Oh __ no. __

You say __ good-bye __ and I say hel - lo, __

125

HELP!

Words and Music by JOHN LENNON
and PAUL McCARTNEY

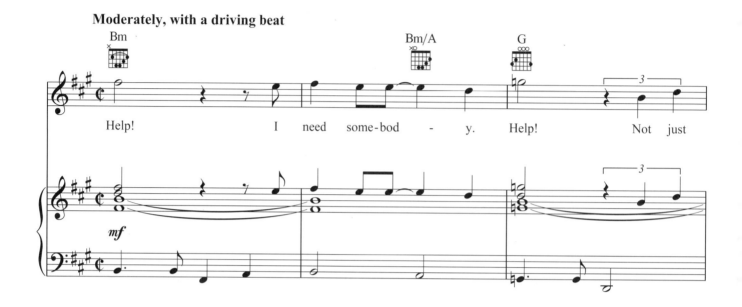

HELTER SKELTER

Words and Music by JOHN LENNON
and PAUL McCARTNEY

Moderate Rock

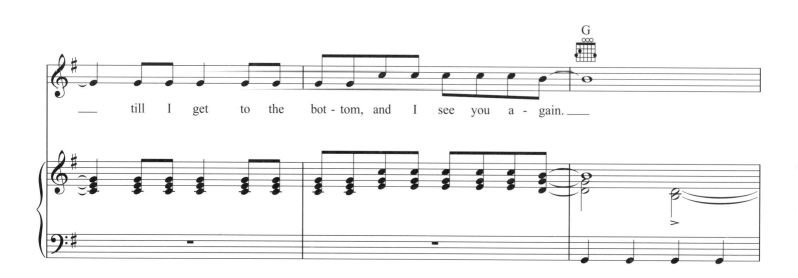

Look out! 'Cause here she comes!

When I get to the bot-tom, I go back to the top of the slide, ___ and I stop and I

HERE COMES THE SUN

Words and Music by
GEORGE HARRISON

Here comes the sun, doo da doo doo,

here comes the sun, and I say, "It's all right."

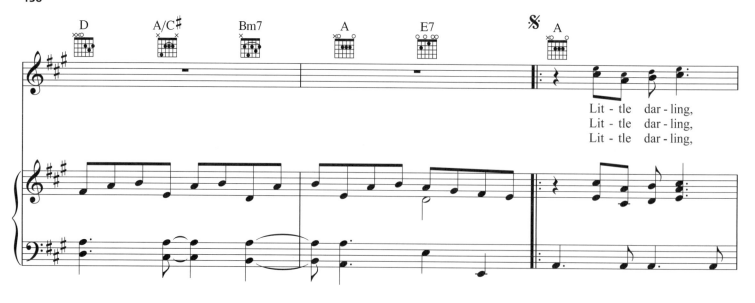

Lit - tle dar - ling,
Lit - tle dar - ling,
Lit - tle dar - ling,

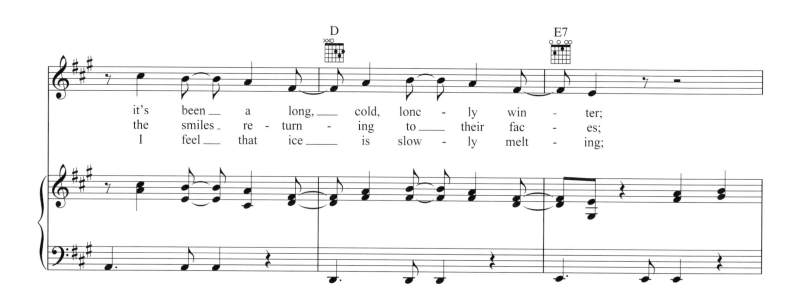

it's been __ a long, __ cold, lone - ly win - ter;
the smiles __ re - turn - ing to __ their fac - es;
I feel __ that ice __ is slow - ly melt - ing;

lit - tle dar - ling, it feels __ like years __ since it's __ been here. __
lit - tle dar - ling, it seems __ like years __ since it's __ been here. __
lit - tle dar - ling, it seems __ like years __ since it's __ been clear. __

Here comes the sun,

here comes the sun, and I say, "It's all right."

To Coda

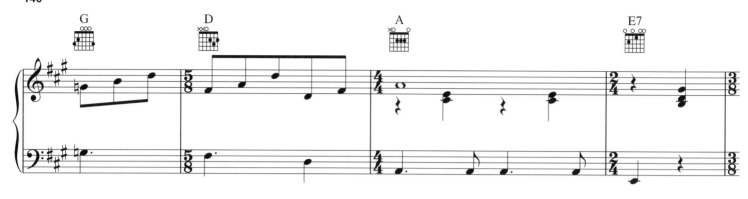

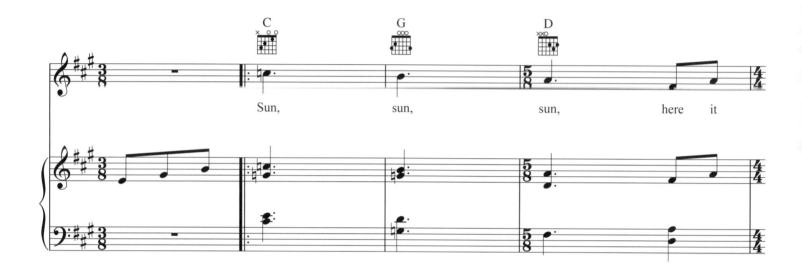

Sun,   sun,   sun,   here   it

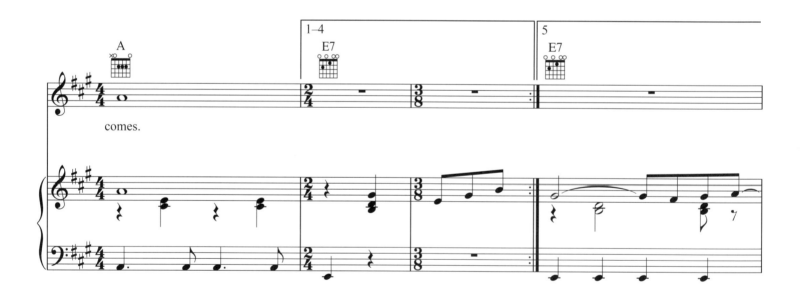

comes.

D.S. al Coda

HEY JUDE

Words and Music by JOHN LENNON
and PAUL McCARTNEY

HONEY PIE

Words and Music by JOHN LENNON
and PAUL McCARTNEY

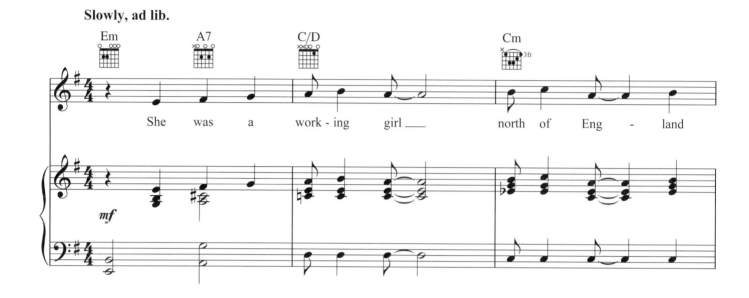

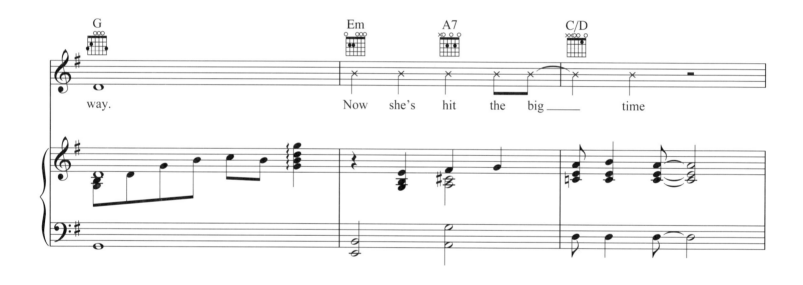

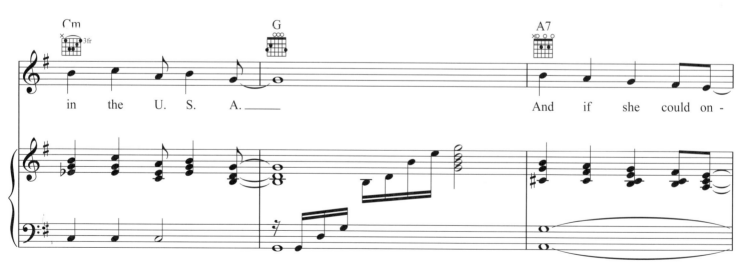

I SHOULD HAVE KNOWN BETTER

Words and Music by JOHN LENNON
and PAUL McCARTNEY

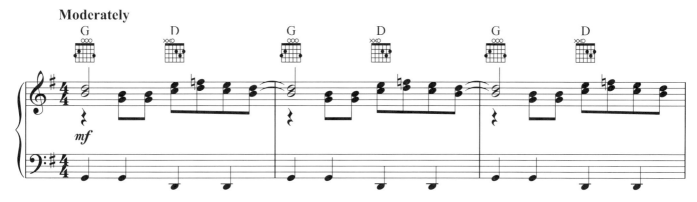

Moderately

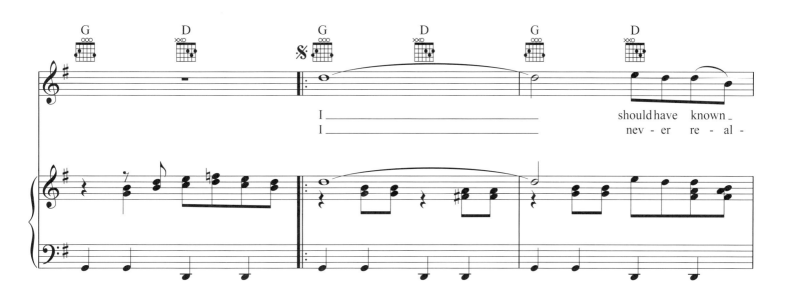

I _____
I _____ should have known _____
nev - er re - al -

bet - ter with a girl like you, _____ that I would love ev - 'ry - thing that you do, _____
ized _____ what a kiss could be, _____ this could on - ly _____ hap - pen to me. _____

I AM THE WALRUS

Words and Music by JOHN LENNON
and PAUL McCARTNEY

I am he as you are he as
Ex- pert tex- pert chok- ing smok- ers,

you are me and we are all to- geth - er.
don't you think the jok- er laughs at you?

I FEEL FINE

Words and Music by JOHN LENNON
and PAUL McCARTNEY

I SAW HER STANDING THERE

Words and Music by JOHN LENNON
and PAUL McCARTNEY

Bright Rock

Well, she was just ____ sev- en- teen, ____ and you
____ looked at me ____ and I, ____

know what I mean, ____ and the way she looked ____ was way ____
____ I could see ____ that be- fore too long ____ I'd

____ be- yond com- pare. ____
____ fall in love with her. ____ So,

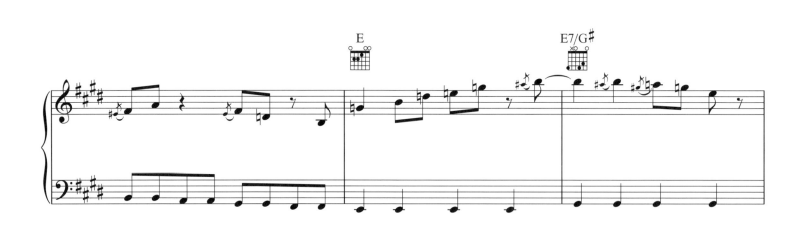

I WANNA BE YOUR MAN

Words and Music by JOHN LENNON
and PAUL McCARTNEY

I wan-na be your man, ___

I WILL

Words and Music by JOHN LENNON
and PAUL McCARTNEY

Who knows ___ how long ___ I've loved ___ you? ___ You know ___ I love ___ you still. ___
___ I ev - er saw ___ you, ___ I did - n't catch ___ your name. ___

Will I wait ___ a lone - ly life - time? If you want ___ me to, ___ I will. ___
But it nev - er real - ly mat - tered; I will al - ways feel ___ the same. ___

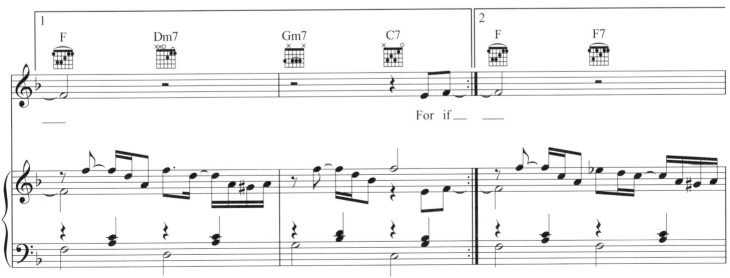

For if ___ ___

I WANT TO HOLD YOUR HAND

Words and Music by JOHN LENNON
and PAUL McCARTNEY

I WANT YOU
(She's So Heavy)

Words and Music by JOHN LENNON
and PAUL McCARTNEY

heav - y, _____ heav - y. _____
heav - y, _____

Instrumental

D.S. al Coda

I want

CODA

She's so

Play 14 times

I'LL BE BACK

Words and Music by JOHN LENNON
and PAUL McCARTNEY

I'LL FOLLOW THE SUN

Words and Music by JOHN LENNON
and PAUL McCARTNEY

sun.)
sun.)
And now the

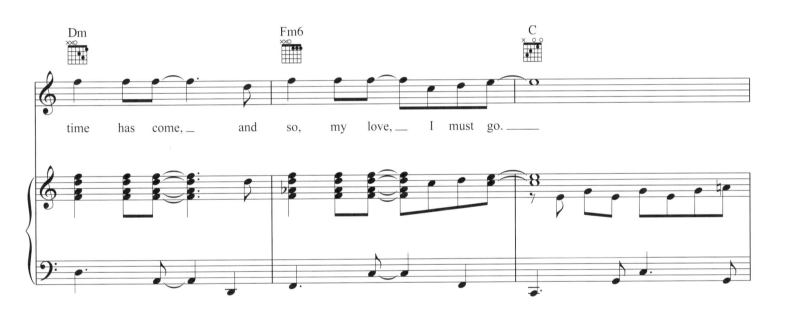

time has come, __ and so, my love, __ I must go. __

And though I lose a friend, __ in the end __ you will know. __

I'M LOOKING THROUGH YOU

Words and Music by JOHN LENNON
and PAUL McCARTNEY

I'm look - ing through __ you,
Your lips are mov -

__ you, where did you go? __
- ing, I can - not __ hear,

I'VE JUST SEEN A FACE

Words and Music by JOHN LENNON
and PAUL McCARTNEY

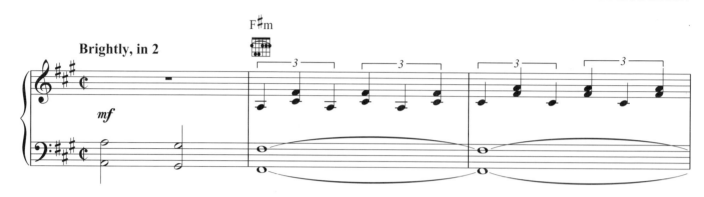

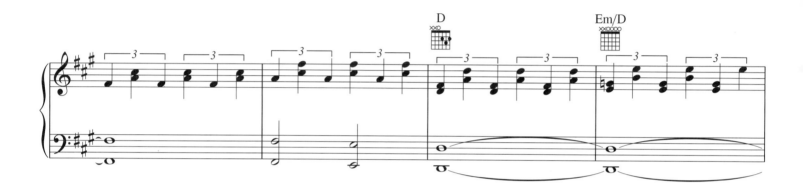

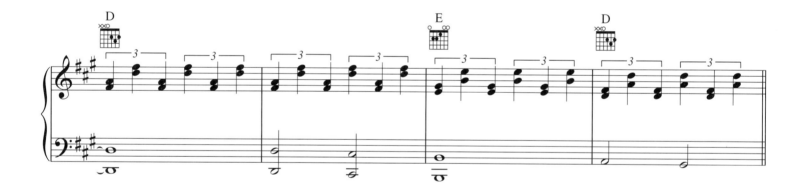

I've just seen a face, I can't for-get the time __ or

IF I FELL

Words and Music by JOHN LENNON
and PAUL McCARTNEY

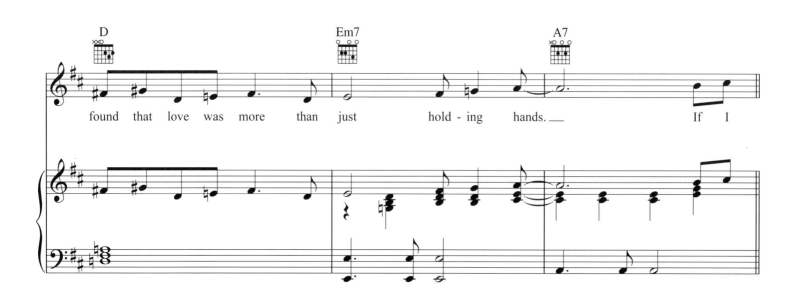

IN MY LIFE

Words and Music by JOHN LENNON
and PAUL McCARTNEY

Moderately

There are plac- es I'll re- mem- ber all my
But of all these friends and lov- ers all there is

life,_____ though some have changed.___ Some for- ev- er, not for
no _____ one com- pares with you.___ And these mem- 'ries lose for their

bet- ter; some have gone _____ and some re- main.__ All these
mean- ing when I think of __ love as some- thing new.__ Tho' I

LET IT BE

Words and Music by JOHN LENNON
and PAUL McCARTNEY

IT WON'T BE LONG

Words and Music by JOHN LENNON
and PAUL McCARTNEY

It won't be long, yeah, (Yeah) yeah, (Yeah) yeah. (Yeah) It won't be

long, — yeah, (Yeah) yeah, (Yeah) yeah. (Yeah) It won't be long, yeah, (Yeah) till

I be - long to you.

216

I'll be good like I know I should, ___ you're com - ing

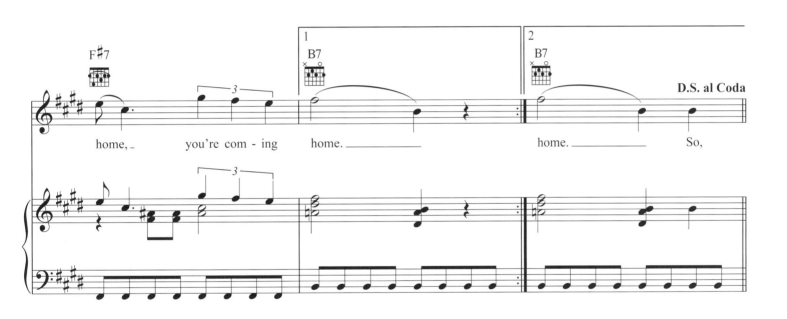

home, _ you're com - ing home. ____ home. ____ So,

D.S. al Coda

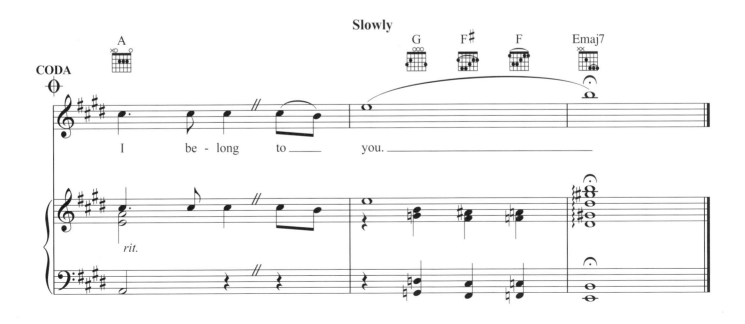

I be - long to ___ you. ____

JULIA

Words and Music by JOHN LENNON
and PAUL McCARTNEY

Moderately slow and wistfully

Half of what I say is mean-ing-less,
When I can-not say sing my heart,

but I say it just to reach you,
I can on-ly speak my mind,

Ju li a,
Ju li-a,

LADY MADONNA

Words and Music by JOHN LENNON
and PAUL McCARTNEY

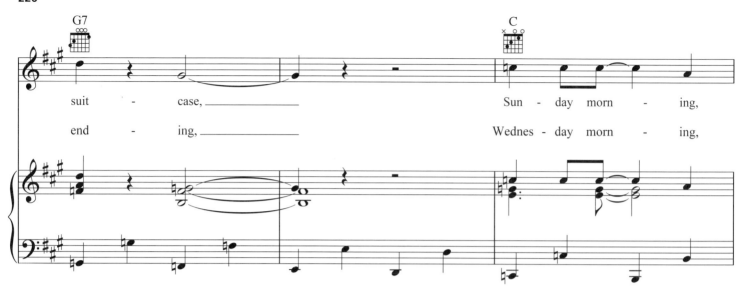

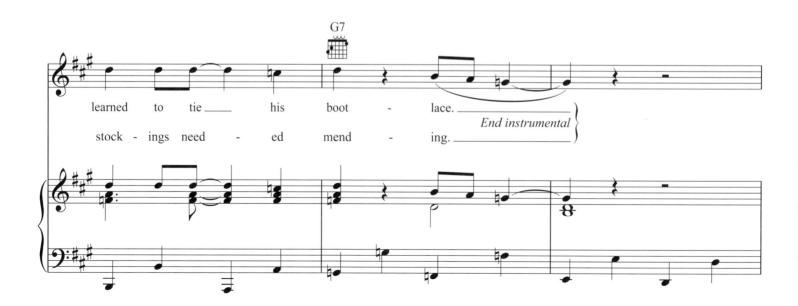

THE LONG AND WINDING ROAD

Words and Music by JOHN LENNON
and PAUL McCARTNEY

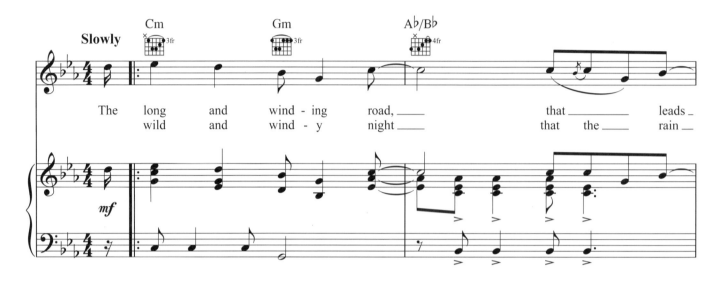

The long and wind-ing road, _____ that _____ leads
wild and wind-y night _____ that the _____ rain

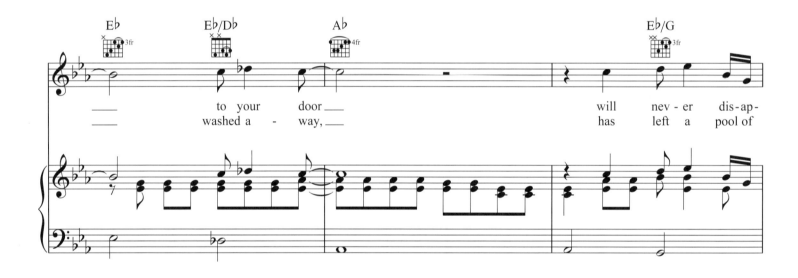

to your door _____
washed a - way, _____
will nev-er dis-ap-
has left a pool of

pear.
tears
I've seen that road be-fore. _____
cry-ing for the day. _____

LOVE ME DO

Words and Music by JOHN LENNON
and PAUL McCARTNEY

Love, love me do, you know I love you. I'll

so please _____ love me

do. _____ Whoa _____ love ___ me do. ___

Repeat and Fade

Whoa _____ love ___ me do. ___

LOVELY RITA

Words and Music by JOHN LENNON
and PAUL McCARTNEY

MARTHA MY DEAR

Words and Music by JOHN LENNON
and PAUL McCARTNEY

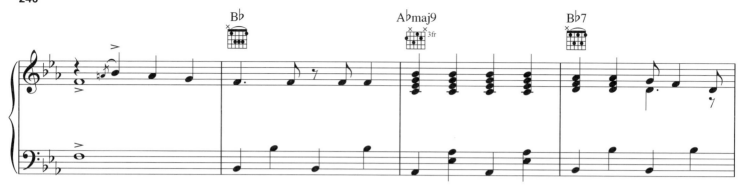

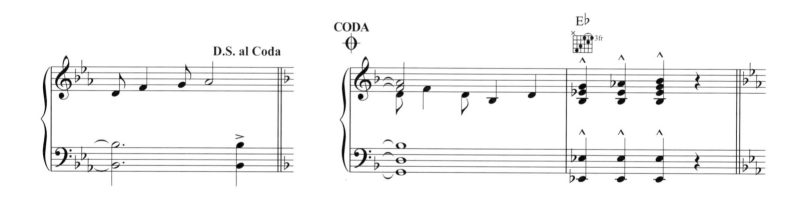

Mar - tha ___ my dear, ___ you have al - ways been my in - spi -

LUCY IN THE SKY WITH DIAMONDS

Words and Music by JOHN LENNON
and PAUL McCARTNEY

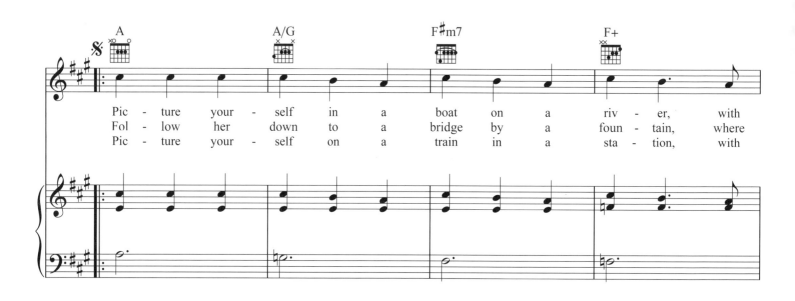

Picture your- self in a boat on a river, with
Fol- low her down to a bridge by a foun- tain, where
Pic- ture your- self on a train in a sta- tion, with

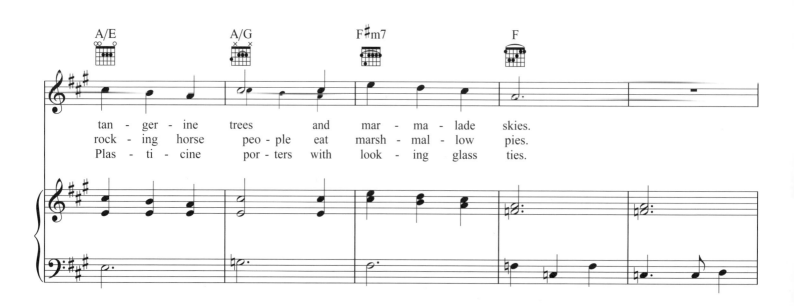

tan- ger- ine trees and mar- ma- lade skies.
rock- ing horse peo- ple eat marsh- mal- low pies.
Plas- ti- cine por- ters with look- ing glass ties.

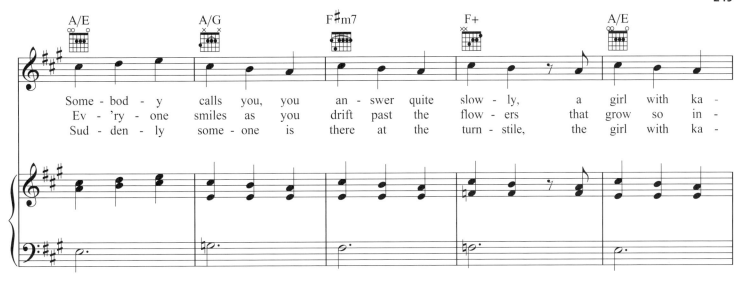

Some-bod-y calls you, you an-swer quite slow-ly, a girl with ka-
Ev-'ry-one smiles as you drift past the flow-ers that grow so in-
Sud-den-ly some-one is there at the turn-stile, the girl with ka-

To Coda

lei - do - scope eyes. _____
cred - i - bly high. _____
lei - do - scope

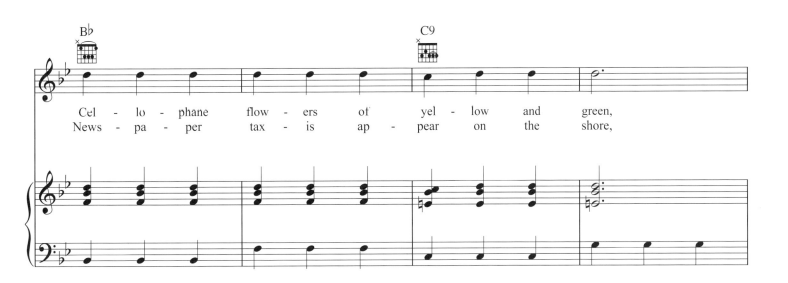

Cel - lo - phane flow - ers of yel - low and green,
News - pa - per tax - is ap - pear on the shore,

MAGICAL MYSTERY TOUR

Words and Music by JOHN LENNON
and PAUL McCARTNEY

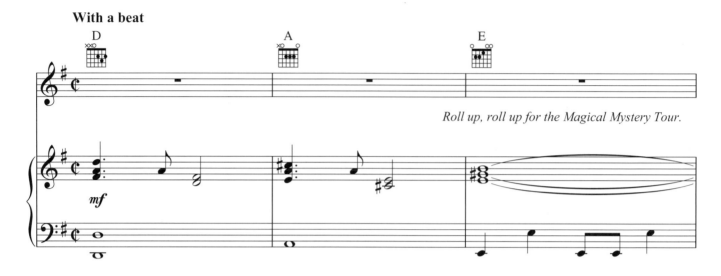

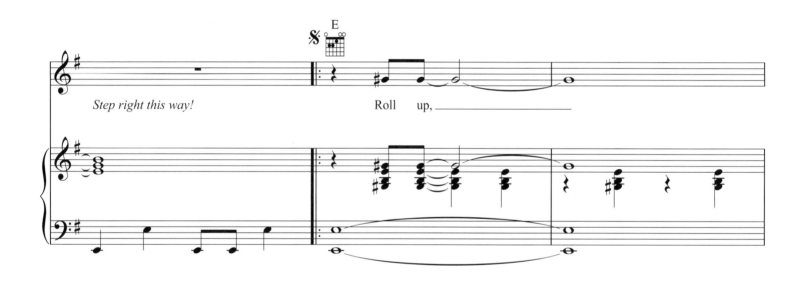

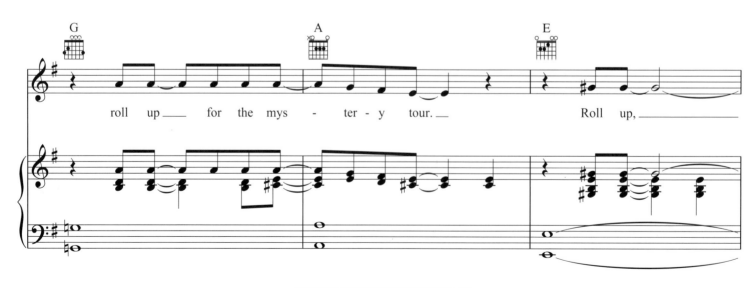

MAXWELL'S SILVER HAMMER

Words and Music by JOHN LENNON
and PAUL McCARTNEY

Joan was quiz-zi-cal, stud-ied pat-a-phys-i-cal sci-ence in the home. _
Back in school a-gain, Max-well plays the fool a-gain. Teach-er gets an-noyed,
P. C. Thir-ty-one said, "We've caught a dir-ty one." Max-well stands a-lone, _

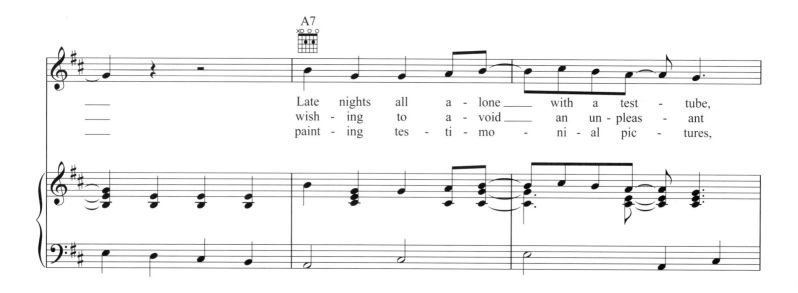

Late nights all a-lone _ with a test-tube,
wish-ing to a-void _ an un-pleas-ant
paint-ing tes-ti-mo-ni-al pic-tures,

oh, oh, oh, oh. _
scene. _
oh, oh, oh, oh. _

Max-well Ed-i-son,
She tells Max to stay
Rose and Val-er-ie

Sil - ver ham - mer.

MICHELLE

Words and Music by JOHN LENNON
and PAUL McCARTNEY

MOTHER NATURE'S SON

Words and Music by JOHN LENNON
and PAUL McCARTNEY

NO REPLY

Words and Music by JOHN LENNON
and PAUL McCARTNEY

Moderately

This hap-pened once be - fore, when I came to your door, no re -
phone, they said you were not home, that's a

ply. _____
lie. _____

They said it was - n't you, but I saw you peep
'Cause I know where you've been, and I saw you walk

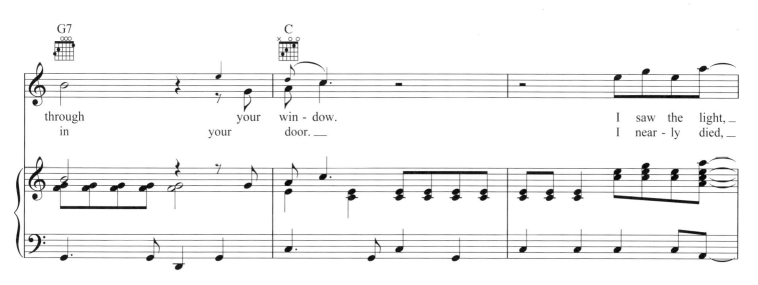

through your win - dow.
in your door. _____

I saw the light, _____
I near - ly died, _____

NORWEGIAN WOOD
(This Bird Has Flown)

Words and Music by JOHN LENNON
and PAUL McCARTNEY

NOWHERE MAN

Words and Music by JOHN LENNON
and PAUL McCARTNEY

He's a real no-where man, sit-ting in ____ his

no-where land, mak-ing all ____ his no-where plans for

no-bod-y.
Does-n't have ____ a
He's as blind ____ as

world _____ is at your com - mand.
some - bod - y else lends you a hand.
world _____ is at your com - mand.

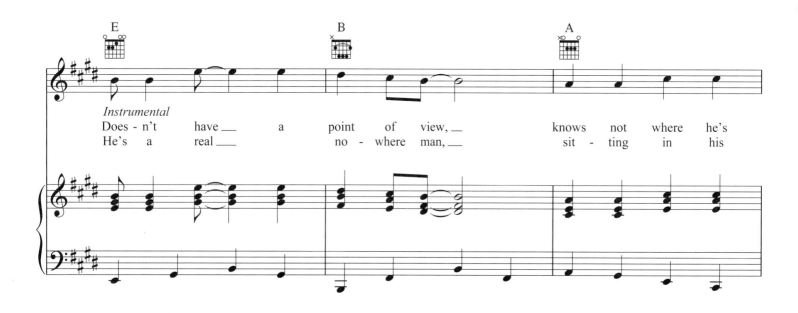

Instrumental

Does - n't have __ a point of view, __ knows not where he's
He's a real __ no - where man, __ sit - ting in his

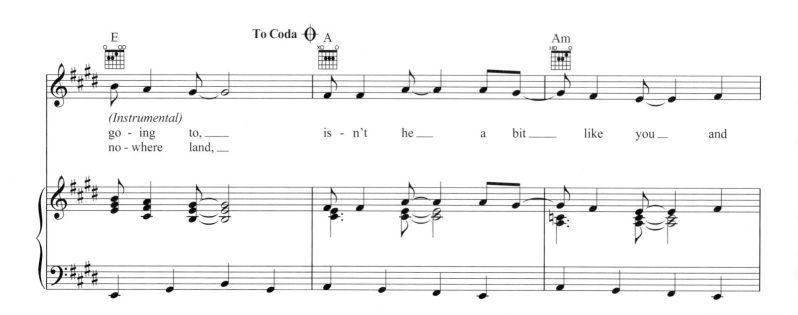

(Instrumental)

go - ing to, ____ is - n't he __ a bit __ like you __ and
no - where land, __

OB-LA-DI, OB-LA-DA

Words and Music by JOHN LENNON
and PAUL McCARTNEY

OCTOPUS'S GARDEN

Words and Music by
RICHARD STARKEY

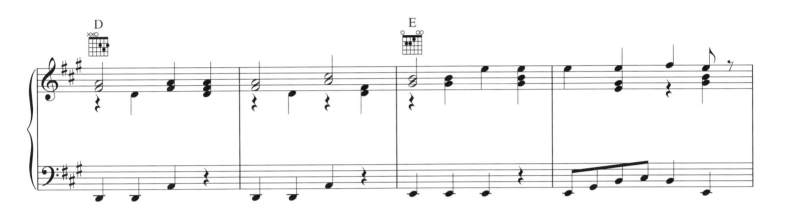

PENNY LANE

Words and Music by JOHN LENNON
and PAUL McCARTNEY

OH! DARLING

Words and Music by JOHN LENNON
and PAUL McCARTNEY

Oh, __ dar - ling, __ please be - lieve me, __
dar - ling, __ if you leave me, __

I'll nev - er do you __ no harm; __
I'll nev - er make it __ a - lone; __

lieve me when I tell you, I'll nev - er do you __ no
lieve me when I beg you, don't ev - er leave me __ a -

be -
be -

P.S. I LOVE YOU

Words and Music by JOHN LENNON
and PAUL McCARTNEY

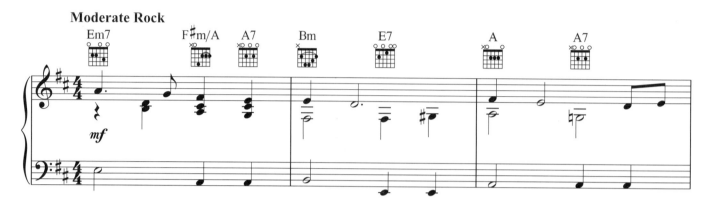

As I write this let-ter,

send my love to you, re-mem-ber that I'll

PAPERBACK WRITER

Words and Music by JOHN LENNON
and PAUL McCARTNEY

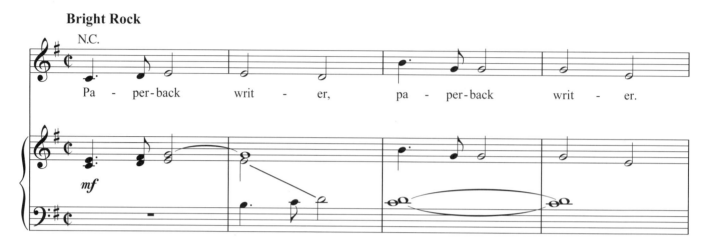

PLEASE PLEASE ME

Words and Music by JOHN LENNON
and PAUL McCARTNEY

Moderately, with a beat

(1.,3.) Last night I said these words to my _____ girl,
(2.) You don't need me to show the way, _____ love.

I know you nev - er e - ven
Why do I al - ways have to

try, _____ girl. }
say, _____ love? }

Come on, (come on,) ____ come

SGT. PEPPER'S LONELY HEARTS CLUB BAND

Words and Music by JOHN LENNON
and PAUL McCARTNEY

Moderately slow, but with a strong beat

REVOLUTION

Words and Music by JOHN LENNON
and PAUL McCARTNEY

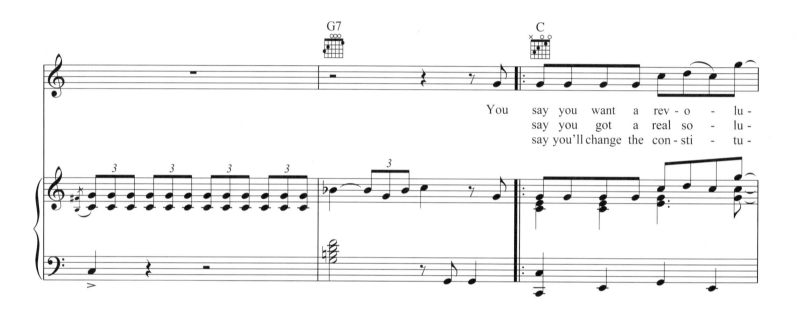

You say you want a rev-o-lu-
say you got a real so-lu-
say you'll change the con-sti-tu-

-tion; _____ well, _____ you know, _____ we all want _
-tion; _____ well, _____ you know, _____ we'd all love _
-tion; _____ well, _____ you know, _____ we all want _

ROCKY RACCOON

Words and Music by JOHN LENNON
and PAUL McCARTNEY

help with good Rock - y's re - viv - al.

RUN FOR YOUR LIFE

Words and Music by JOHN LENNON
and PAUL McCARTNEY

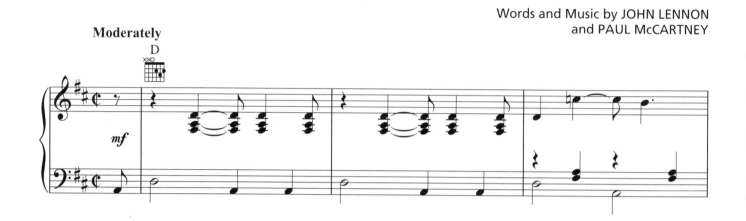

Well, I'd

rath - er see you dead, ___ lit - tle girl, than to be with an - oth - er man. ___
know that I'm a wick - ed guy and I was born with a jeal - ous mind. ___
Let this be a ser - mon, I mean ev - 'ry - thing ___ I said. ___
rath - er see you dead, ___ lit - tle girl, than to be with an - oth - er man. ___

SEXY SADIE

Words and Music by JOHN LENNON
and PAUL McCARTNEY

SHE LOVES YOU

Words and Music by JOHN LENNON
and PAUL McCARTNEY

Moderately

She loves you, yeah, yeah, yeah. She loves you, yeah,

yeah, yeah. She loves you, yeah, yeah, yeah, yeah.

You think you've lost your love? Well, I

SHE'S A WOMAN

Words and Music by JOHN LENNON
and PAUL McCARTNEY

Fairly bright, with a strong back beat

(1.,3.,D.S.) My love don't give me pres-ents,
(2.) She don't give boys the eye.____

I know that she's no peas-ant.
She hates to see me cry.____

D.S. al Coda

CODA

Repeat and Fade

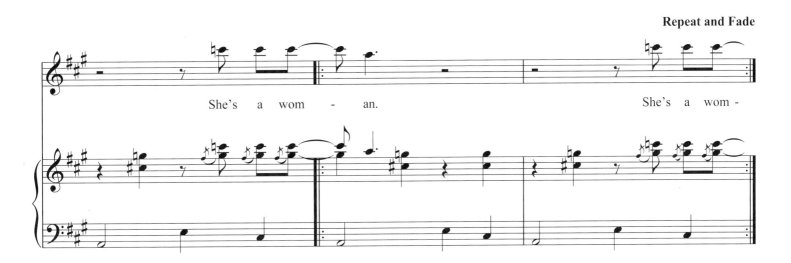

SHE'S LEAVING HOME

Words and Music by JOHN LENNON
and PAUL McCARTNEY

SOMETHING

Words and Music by
GEORGE HARRISON

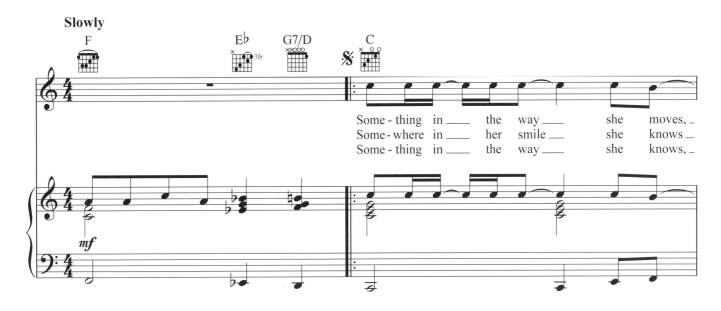

Some-thing in ___ the way ___ she moves, ___
Some-where in ___ her smile ___ she knows ___
Some-thing in ___ the way ___ she knows, ___

at - tracts ___ me like ___ no oth-er lov - er.
that I ___ don't need ___ no oth-er lov - er.
and all ___ I have ___ to do is think ___ of her.

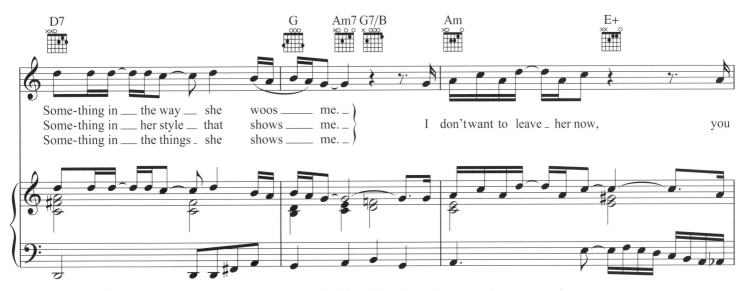

Some-thing in ___ the way ___ she woos ___ me. ___
Some-thing in ___ her style ___ that shows ___ me. ___
Some-thing in ___ the things ___ she shows ___ me. ___

I don't want to leave ___ her now,   you

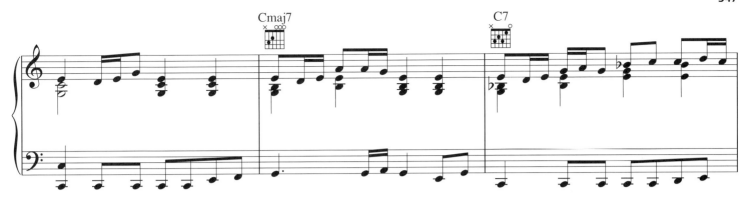

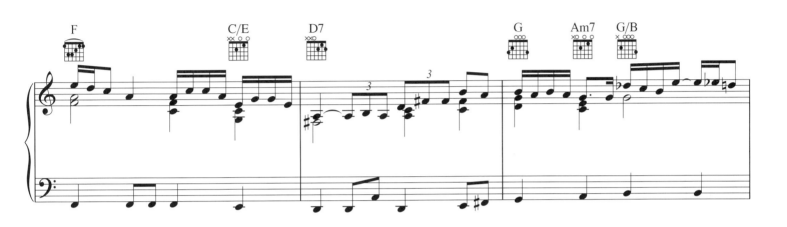

D.S. al Coda

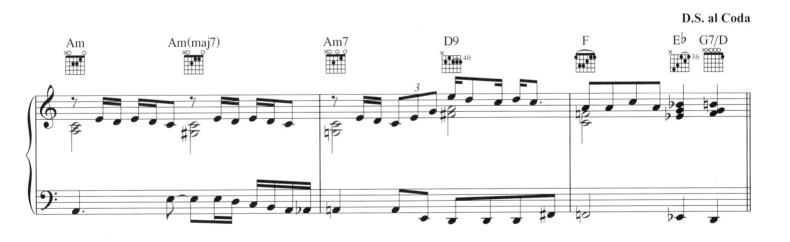

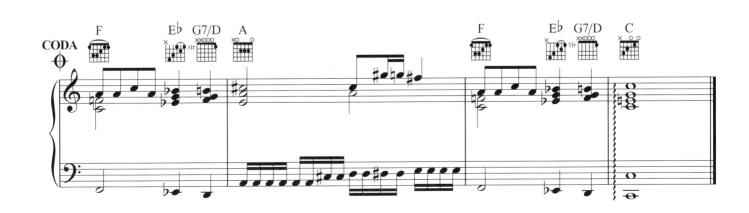

STRAWBERRY FIELDS FOREVER

Words and Music by JOHN LENNON
and PAUL McCARTNEY

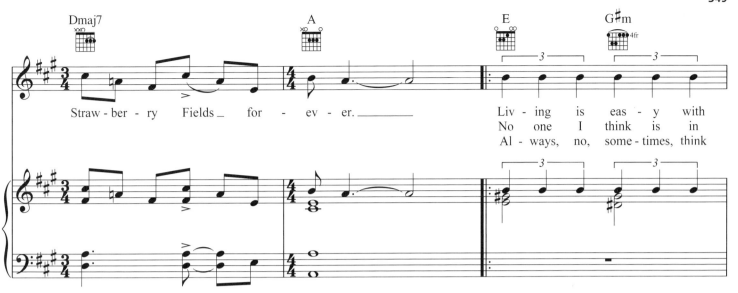

one, but it all ___ works ___ out;   it does-n't mat-ter much to
in, but it's all ___ right.   That is, I think it's not too
"Yes," but it's all _____ wrong.   That is, I think I dis-a-

me. }
bad. }   Let me take you down, ___ 'cause I'm go-ing to ___
gree. }

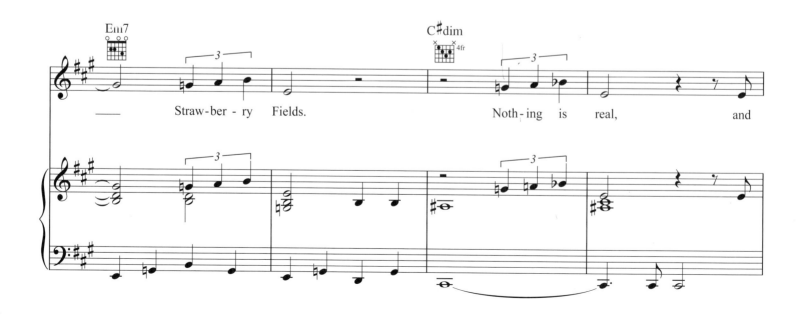

___ Straw-ber-ry Fields.   Noth-ing is real,   and

TAXMAN

Words and Music by
GEORGE HARRISON

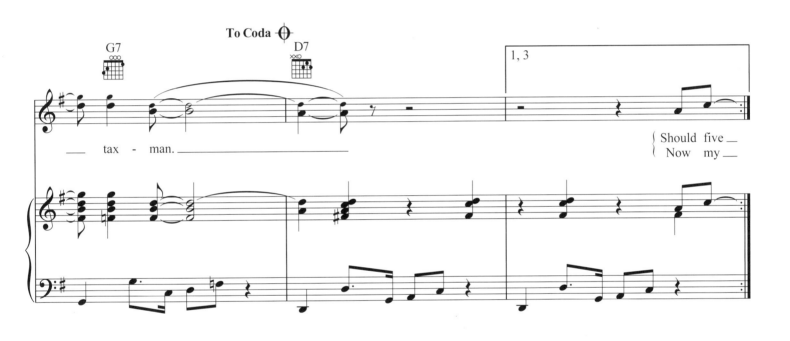

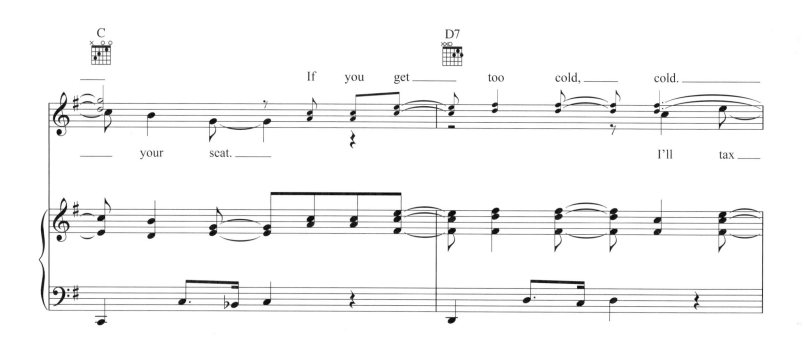

WE CAN WORK IT OUT

Words and Music by JOHN LENNON
and PAUL McCARTNEY

Try to see it my way, do I have to keep on talk-ing
Think of what you're say - ing, you can get it wrong and still you

till I can't go on? While you see it your way, run the risk of know-ing that our
think that it's al - right. Think of what I'm say - ing, we can work it out and get it

love may soon be gone. } We can work it out, we can work it out. _____
straight, or say good - night. }

TELL ME WHY

Words and Music by JOHN LENNON
and PAUL McCARTNEY

THINGS WE SAID TODAY

Words and Music by JOHN LENNON
and PAUL McCARTNEY

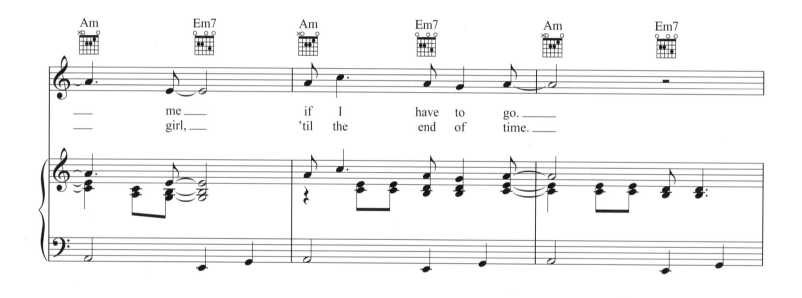

Some - day _____ when I'm lone - ly _____
Some - day _____ when we're dream - ing _____

wish - ing you ___ weren't so far a - way, ___ then I will re - mem -
deep in love, ___ not a lot to say, ___ then we will re - mem -

- ber __ things we said to - day. _____
- ber __ things we said to - day. _____

Me, I'm just ___ the luck - y kind, ___

TICKET TO RIDE

Words and Music by JOHN LENNON
and PAUL McCARTNEY

TWIST AND SHOUT

Words and Music by BERT RUSSELL
and PHIL MEDLEY

Moderately, with a beat

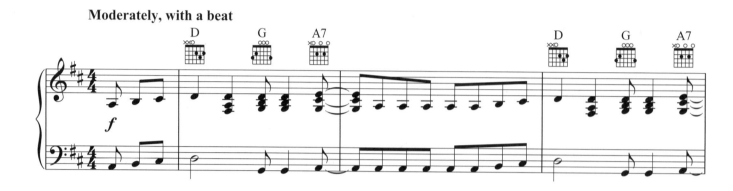

Well, shake it up, ba - by, __ now,
 - by, __ now, } (Shake it up, ba - by) twist and
 - by, __ now,

shout. _____ (Twist and shout) _____ Come on, come on, __ come on, __ come on,

WHEN I'M SIXTY-FOUR

Words and Music by JOHN LENNON
and PAUL McCARTNEY

WHILE MY GUITAR GENTLY WEEPS

Words and Music by
GEORGE HARRISON

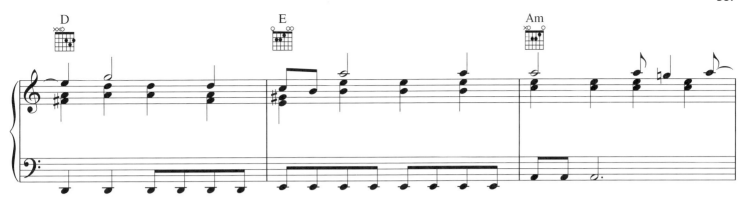

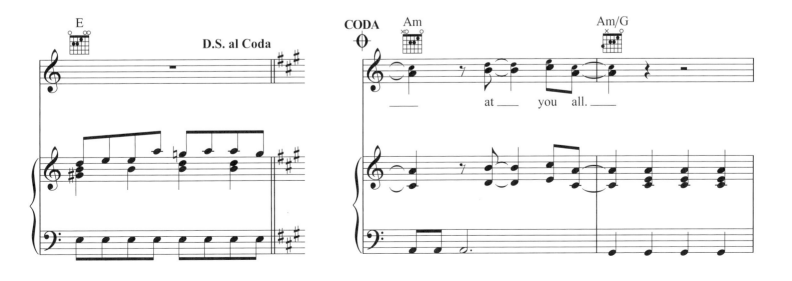

YESTERDAY

Words and Music by JOHN LENNON
and PAUL McCARTNEY

Moderately, with expression

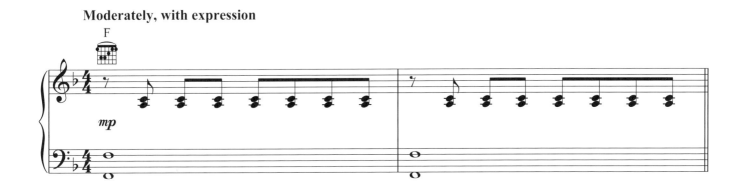

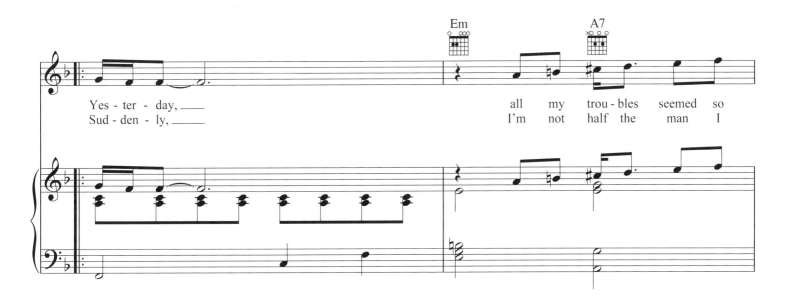

Yes - ter - day, _____ all my trou - bles seemed so
Sud - den - ly, _____ I'm not half the man I

far a - way, _____ now it looks as though ____ they're
used to be, _____ there's a shad - ow hang - ing

WITH A LITTLE HELP FROM MY FRIENDS

Words and Music by JOHN LENNON
and PAUL McCARTNEY

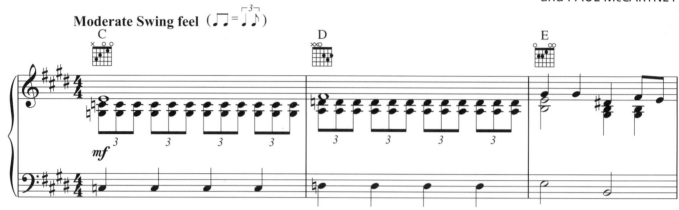

What would you think __ if I sang __ out of tune, __ would you stand __
What do I do __ when my love __ is a-way? __ (Does it wor-
(Would you be-lieve __ in a love __ at first sight?) __ Yes, I'm cer-

__ up and walk __ out on me? __
-ry you to be a-lone?) __
-tain that it hap-pens all the time.

Lend me your ears __ and I'll sing __
How do I feel __ by the end __
(What do you see __ when you turn __

you a song, ____ and I'll try ____ not to sing ____ out of key. ____
of the day? ____ (Are you sad ____ be - cause you're on ____ your own?) ____
out the light?) ____ I can't tell ____ you, but I know ____ it's mine. ____

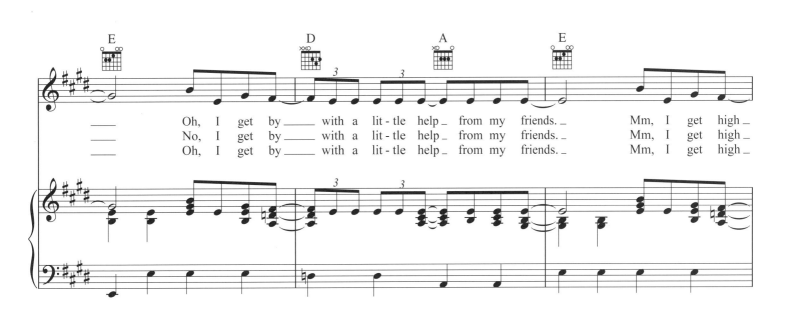

Oh, I get by ____ with a lit - tle help _ from my friends. _ Mm, I get high _
No, I get by ____ with a lit - tle help _ from my friends. _ Mm, I get high _
Oh, I get by ____ with a lit - tle help _ from my friends. _ Mm, I get high _

____ with a lit - tle help ____ from my friends. ____ Mm, I'm gon - na try ____
____ with a lit - tle help ____ from my friends. ____ Mm, I'm gon - na try ____
____ with a lit - tle help ____ from my friends. ____ Oh, I'm gon - na try ____

YELLOW SUBMARINE

Words and Music by JOHN LENNON
and PAUL McCARTNEY

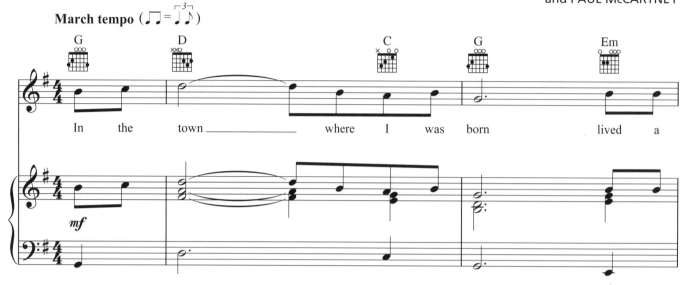

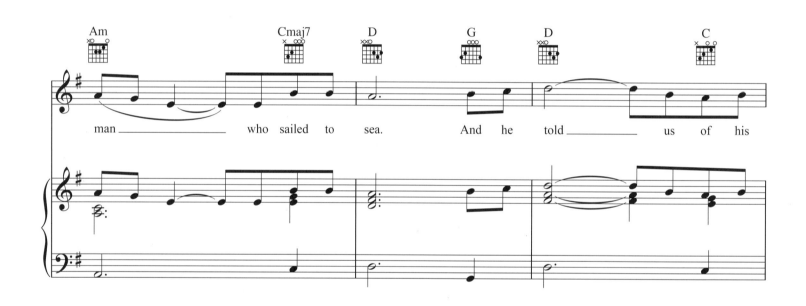

You've Got To Hide Your Love Away

Words and Music by JOHN LENNON
and PAUL McCARTNEY

YOUR MOTHER SHOULD KNOW

Words and Music by JOHN LENNON
and PAUL McCARTNEY

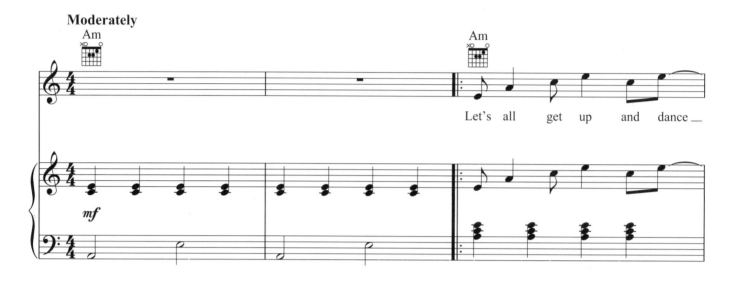

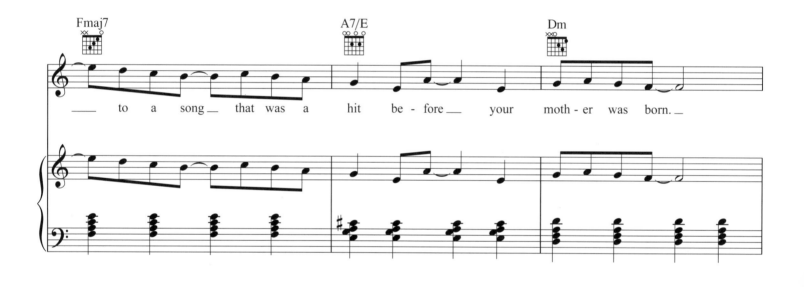

YOU WON'T SEE ME

Words and Music by JOHN LENNON
and PAUL McCARTNEY

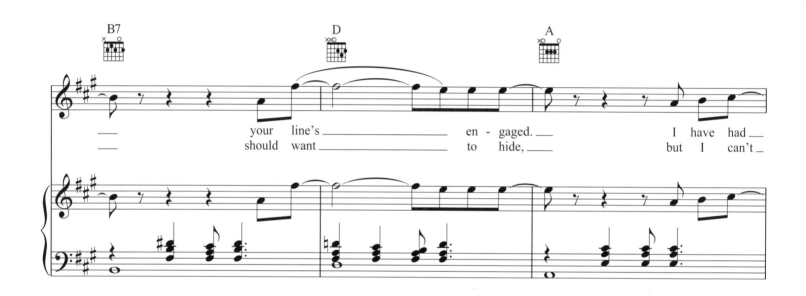

YOU NEVER GIVE ME YOUR MONEY

Words and Music by JOHN LENNON
and PAUL McCARTNEY

One sweet dream, _____

pick up the bags and get in the lim-ou-sine. __

Soon we'll be a-way__ from here, __ step on the gas and wipe__ that tear a-way, __

SUN KING

Words and Music by JOHN LENNON
and PAUL McCARTNEY

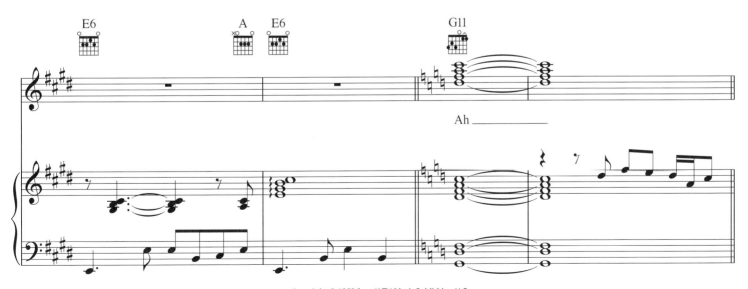

MEAN MR. MUSTARD

Words and Music by JOHN LENNON
and PAUL McCARTNEY

Segue to "Polythene Pam"

POLYTHENE PAM

Words and Music by JOHN LENNON
and PAUL McCARTNEY

Segue to "She Came In Through the Bathroom Window"

SHE CAME IN THROUGH THE BATHROOM WINDOW

Words and Music by JOHN LENNON
and PAUL McCARTNEY

GOLDEN SLUMBERS

Words and Music by JOHN LENNON
and PAUL McCARTNEY

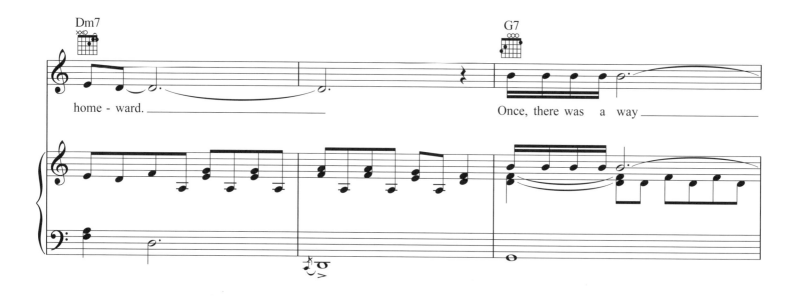

CARRY THAT WEIGHT

Words and Music by JOHN LENNON
and PAUL McCARTNEY

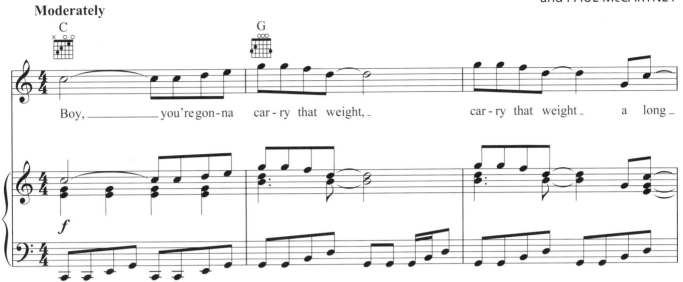

Boy, _____ you're gon-na car-ry that weight, _ car-ry that weight _ a long _

_ time. Boy, _____ you're gon-na car-ry that weight, _

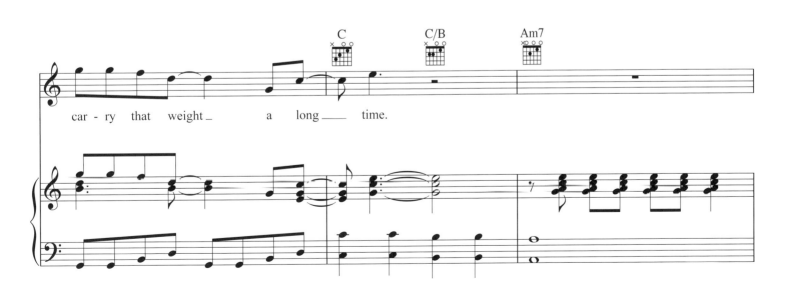

car-ry that weight _ a long _ time.

THE END

Words and Music by JOHN LENNON
and PAUL McCARTNEY

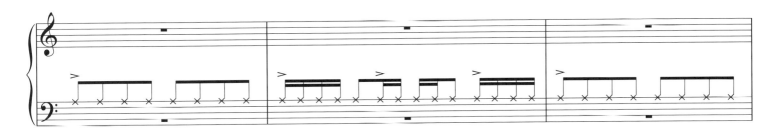

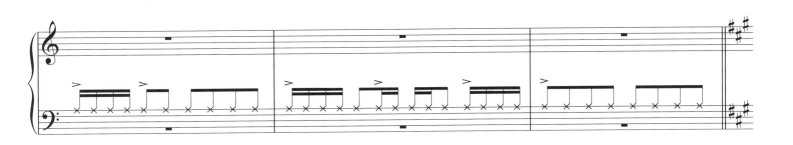

Love you, — love you, —